My Public Letter To Donald Trump

Geeta Chopra

Table of Contents

Dedication

This book is dedicated to the 45th president of the United States, Donald J. Trump. He has broken barriers and kicked down walls that have held American interests back for decades. He is a timeless hero to the American people, and this book is dedicated to the American dream.

Foreword

In this book, Geeta Chopra, extols the accomplishments of our 45th President, Donald Trump and elaborates on his leadership style, accomplishments, and legacy. Geeta addresses his fiscal conservatism, foreign policy, as well as border security. I recommend this book as it brings to light many of the issues that we are facing in the country with a look toward a brighter future.

Senator Doug Mastriano, Ph.D.

Pennsylvania, 33rd District

Just like a gourmet meal, Geeta has expressed her monumental, main-course passion for America with a side order of disappointment, frustration, amazement, and the best dessert of all: Hope. There is no doubt in my mind that Donald J. Trump was selected to be our 45th president by none other than the Man Himself, God. After Trump's stunning election in 2016, I realized that God really does love America. What happened in 2020? Choose almost any book in the Bible to find despair, grief, tumult and loss of hope. And then, redemption. As I try to rationalize the current debacle that America is in the middle of, it's like the winter season; the cold weather and dismal landscape helps us to appreciate the rebirth of spring and the warm days of summer. Thank you, Geeta, for your putting to paper the feelings that I and the many millions of fellow Americaloving Patriots feel. Not only can we relate, we share your hope for the future. God bless the U.S.A

Len   Young,   Chairman   Monroeville   Republican Committee

Acknowledgments

I would like to acknowledge our founding fathers, including but not limited to George Washington, John Adams, Thomas Jefferson, James Madison, Benjamin Franklin, Henry Patrick, Samuel Adams, Alexander Hamilton, and Abigail Adams.

Then again, countless other heroes, such as Abraham Lincoln, Ronald Reagan, JFK, George Bush, Ron DeSantis, Tim Scott, Mike Pence, and finally, Donald Trump, should be acknowledged. These are the individuals who have fought long and hard to maintain the freedom of the American people. Some have died in their quest to do so, while others are relentlessly pursuing it. I would also like to acknowledge those who are currently fighting for America's restoration through prayer and ongoing resilience. Our police force and military, along with additional blue lives, deserve credit for all of their hard work and willingness to lay down their lives for another, especially during these challenging times. God bless all who have died for American freedom. Finally, those who will not let the government dictate their personal choices in an effort to preserve their own God-given freedom, congratulations to you.

Most importantly, without our founding fathers, we would not be here today. Let us stand for what they died to give us.

"For if you do not stand firm in your faith, you will not stand at all."

- Isaiah 7:9

About the Author

Geeta Chopra is a born-again Christian who says Jesus Christ saved her life. She is the television show host of 'We The People' and 'The Abundant Life' at Princeton television network. She also hosted The Scripture of the Day with Geeta at Sakshi TV. She is passionate about her faith and writes Christian books and delivers motivational talks.

Part of her ministry work includes a diploma in mental health counseling from Light University and Christian leadership classes at Allison Park church. With the core belief of God's grace for mankind, she has served as a prayer minister with the 700 Club and the national prayer and crisis center. Geeta serves on the board at the YWCA and dedicates her time to volunteering for several organizations including PRISM, Cornerstone Ministries, and The Lord's church. As a frequent guest speaker at The Rotary Club of New Jersey and the SBA, Geeta gives presentations on the art of negotiation for all. She has spent quite a bit of time in the private sector where she opened her own restaurant and hired, trained, and managed 35 employees at a time. Geeta teaches macroeconomic and microeconomic classes at the college level to follow her passion for fiscal conservatism. In addition, she has a real estate development company. Geeta attributes all of her success to Jesus Christ, who saved her life in every way.

Having grown up in several states in a simpler time, her passion is to make America *America* again. In 2018, she won the governor's award of New Jersey for outstanding public service. She is a patriot of America and stands for the flag. She has a master's degree in International Policy And Practicum from The Elliott School of International Affairs at The George Washington University, and a bachelor's degree in Political Science and Economics from the University of Toronto.

My Public Letter To Donald Trump

"Let him without sin cast the first stone."

Dear Mr. Donald J. Trump, the 45th President of the United States of America.

The good Lord gave me a vision of you in a dream back in January 2021, the inauguration month. Just days before passing the baton to the socialist party of America, I was shown your state of being in a very descriptive manner just around 3:00 a.m. Just like all visions, the key takeaway is always the intense emotion felt during the process of conveying the message from the Holy Spirit. The feeling is what stays. I woke up very disturbed and certainly changed. I didn't view the state of affairs in Washington, DC, the same way after January 2021.

Just weeks earlier, during the tumultuous season of campaigning, a friend sent me a brief YouTube video about you, which piqued my interest. I watched it so intently and took in each word. The man in the video was prophet Sadhu Sundar Selvaraj, and he was discussing your candidacy. I must admit, my first thought towards this man was judgment. I had automatically erroneously assumed due to the race of this individual, he was a hater. He was East Indian, so I assumed he was a liberal who had posted yet another video on why republicans are racists and that perhaps you are their

1

racist leader. However, something in me compelled me to play it. Later, I realized why the Holy Spirit sent it to me. Firstly, this man was an ardent follower of Jesus Christ; and had the gift of prophecy. Secondly, he understood the social conservative biblical values that the republican party represents and the fiscal conservatism it upholds. He was a believer and a fellow patriot of the United States just like you and just like me. He was praying for you while holding back tears.

In the video, the Indian prophet spoke vehemently, choking back emotions of sincere viable concern for the future of America. Being a prophet, he described how America was clearly at a crossroads and all eyes were on the 2020 election. This included all the angels in heaven and the demons of destruction. He described it with such terror that I watched it twice. What happens in November of 2020 will determine the course of the future of the world, he proclaimed. He then went on to describe how you were a man broken because your own party had so many traitors. This is the part that left an indelible memory on my heart. The very people who were supposed to stand by you were nowhere to be found when the house of cards came folding down. Yet, you were still standing strong, fighting for America. God had anointed you to do such an important job. Although you felt as if the world was coming crashing down on you, both figuratively and literally, God had sent three tall, magnificent three-dimensional angels in the spirit to make you don't fall. Perhaps this was the only thing that provided me with a sense of relief. He then proceeded to describe in detail what The Holy Spirit told him about you in his vision of you. Prophet Selvaraj spoke that Donald Trump is a broken man; because his *own* party is against him. Although we witness this in politics frequently, this division was at such a developed level that one could not imagine the evil one man is fighting. It was demonic in nature, a stronghold placed by the enemy of mankind to take down America.

See, it's one thing to have the opposite political party sabotaging every move you make, hold rallies against you, utilize the fake news media to promote their political agenda such as critical race theory, opening borders, NATO, the public welfare state, defunding law enforcement, failing to punish the guilty, and challenging our first amendment along with our second amendment. All of these action items are expected in a fierce political campaign, especially to the party that is, unfortunately, being influenced by socialism. One might depict them undoing the laborious work our founding fathers did in the 1700s to provide for our everyday liberties today. We have uprisings and groups daily challenging the constitution, along with the left-leaning party challenging the second and now first amendment. We have seen all this, and we have become nauseated.

However, when this man spoke about you being the only one with courage in the republican party standing up for justice and fighting desperately to uphold its original values, he got my attention. This was a punch from left field that we weren't expecting in 2020. He said in attempting to keep the party together in the hope of sustaining our bedrock principles; your spirit was challenged. There you were, fighting evil. The bible teaches us that no human is the enemy; the enemy is the true enemy of the brethren, and he seeks to separate and divide mankind. He works through willing people who will let him in. He described the brokenness you felt as a human when people you had counted on simply vanished into thin air.

I believe you were fighting a spiritual battle. The battle was not of the flesh, and the enemy of mankind wanted to destroy America. It is important to remember as humans that flesh is not the enemy. Equally as important, and frightening, in the video, he described the destruction that he believed God said would take place in America if you did not get elected again for another four years. China rising from the East, Russia coming in from the west, terrorists arriving through our southern border, and our enemies taking advantage of us (Fast forward to today, some of those visions have already started to come to pass). Of course we welcome immigrants and refugees through our borders, but opening up to terrorist attacks is plain foolish. Next, the bedrock morals that America has stood on for 200 years in terms of economic liberty and free speech would be challenged and blown into dust within the first year. Of course, now we see this with pregnant men, unprecedented transgenderism, and civil rights issues surrounding the pronoun of a person, all of which distort the original structure of the human gender and are satanic in nature. What the left is doing with gender identity is against the word of God and unnatural, along with many other frightening, ungodly policies.

However, that is the least of our worries given the ongoing invasion of the southern border by criminals posing as refugees; who then spoil it for the true refugees, a lack of a border, a crashing currency, rampant inflation, high unemployment, wage inflation, supply chain shortages, increasing abortions, identity politics, racial tensions rising, and failed foreign policy abroad coupled with wasteful trade agreements and a loss of power on the international stage.

"Every post is honorable in which a man can serve his country."

-George Washington

My Vision

Coming back to what the Lord showed me, needless to say, I was very disturbed. A few weeks later, just weeks after the election, the Holy Spirit expressly spoke to me in a dream about you. He showed me in the spirit, in such an emotional manner, how the days after the election results, you were fighting an unimaginable evil. You alone were fighting a group of people that you had worked with for years prior, and they had all turned their back to you. This message was conveyed to me visually, and it tore me apart. There was an image of you at a table with the same people you had hosted. In this dream, the Lord showed me how you went to each guest one by one that you so graciously hosted with your own funds to ask them for support during the most challenging time of your life – the 2020 elections. You had just spent the last four years building back America, strengthening our economy, bringing back manufacturing jobs for the middle class, lowering taxes, withdrawing America from trade agreements that we had nothing to gain from, built the wall, mobilized our military, cleaned up corruption at the government level, passed prison reform, created thousands of jobs, and so much more. There is not one patriotic American who did not benefit from what you did.

Now, at this table, you asked these players for support.

These were the same people you fought for! One by one, they all turned their face to you in a shameful manner. Their faces turned ice-cold as if possessed by something. You were flying back and forth in the room but couldn't find relief. A picture of you flying from one seat to the next in search of an ally plagued me that night. It was the ultimate betrayal. God showed me your pain, and it haunted me for weeks to follow.

I believe those players in the dream partly represented the supreme court, congress, senate, the senate majority leader, social media, and others from your own cabinet. The symbolism of a dinner table was perhaps personified the last supper, just before they would crucify you. It also refreshed me with Psalm 23:5, where King David stated that the Lord prepares a table for you in the presence of your enemies. God will use this to somehow deliver things – even better. I truly believe that. The journey there is where we are currently. The chinaware was marvelous to take in, and the ambiance was beautiful. However, the betrayal overtook the aesthetics, and a feeling of somberness permeated the picture. I was very disturbed.

Additionally, some Christians from the left have done the very thing that God condemns: judged you. I have heard Christians say that due to your personal behaviors or preferences, they cannot endorse you. This is in direct contradiction to Romans chapter two. It is important for them to recall that God uses the same yardstick as a measurement to judge them once they have judged another. Furthermore, the book of Romans clarifies that when we judge someone else, we become part of (under) the law and are judged accordingly.

You, therefore, have no excuse, you who pass judgment on someone else, for at whatever point you judge another, you are condemning yourself, because you who pass judgment do the same things.[2] Now we know that God's judgment against those who do such things is based on truth.[3] So when you, a mere human being, pass judgment on them and yet do the same things, do you think you will escape God's judgment?[4] Or do you show contempt for the riches of his kindness, forbearance, and patience, not realizing that God's kindness is intended to lead you to repentance?

This last election year was not an election year. I believe it was a time to vote for the life or death of America. It was a time for Americans to decide if we wanted to save our country or give it to the enemy. I still believe you won, and you are my president. Having lived in socialist Canada throughout my 30s, I know firsthand the destructive tendencies of a controlling government on its people. Sadly, because most Americans don't know this experience, they deny its existence and evil implications. Growing up in America as a child and teenager, I never knew the pitfalls of socialism until I spent time in Canada. When the government has more power over the people, socialism is born. Now, some Americans do not understand this concept, and it has become a dangerous threat to our future as a free nation with the most enriching, rewarding constitution in the world. America, I am blessed beyond all measure, and I pray that all Americans see this one day before it's too late.

"A government big enough to give you everything you want is strong enough to take away everything you have."

Only in our fallen world would people rebel against the very mother-hand that nourishes them. Humans are a peculiar species worth examining. You wanted to save America from southern invasions, such as terrorists disguised as refugees and individuals who come here and undercut American wages by working for ten cents on the dollar per hour with no breaks. Not to mention Hezbollah and countless additional terrorist groups sneaking through them as they come to murder Americans and blow up our buildings. You fought hard to bring back manufacturing jobs that succumbed to China and other countries due to imbalanced trade agreements, and you spoke vigorously on protecting American interests abroad and at home. China has been dumping steel into America for decades until you took a courageous stand against that. Many nations have plundered economically and politically, including the

NATO group. After years of political enslavement, Americans were starving for a leader who would stand up to China for unfair trade practices, against countries that take and give nothing back, protect our border from crime and injustice. Even if certain voters did not endorse you personally, certainly they can still make the healthier choice for our country's future. At one point, the only logical conclusion one could derive after studying your campaign and presidency in detail is that those who were against you were haters of America. But, God, how could that be true? I cannot believe those people hate America, so this remains a paradox that I have prayed for deeper insight into.

Your presidency was unique to America for several reasons, and perhaps the highlighting pinnacle was that it separated the patriots from the enemy within. Who knew there was a group of flag-burning statues demolishing haters in our own land? Thank you for bringing these infidels to the surface and exposing them. I realized that you are fighting an evil none of us can imagine. Your supporters are with you in the fight. Let us pray for all Americans during this time and ask God to impart wisdom to all of us. And we shall overcome.

"Let us, therefore, rely upon the goodness of the Cause, and the aid of the Supreme Being, in whose hands Victory is, to animate and encourage us to be great and noble Actions—the eyes of all our countrymen are now upon us."

-George Washington

I don't believe you are racist. I qualify myself to make this statement as a woman of color! On January 1, 1863, when Abraham Lincoln signed the emancipation proclamation, I am sure it was met with resistance. However, I doubt a single black American resisted it. Today, we find ourselves in a peculiar time and age of cognitive dissonance. No wonder masses of people protest against your policies. As a general rule, people don't like change, especially the entitled. When you have humans deeply entrenched in the dependency system of government reliance for decades, when someone offers a way out and into self-reliance, of course, the first instinct is to resist.

God used you to bring true, tangible, undeniable change beyond a reasonable doubt. He performed miracles for America through you and shattered chains that have kept us in political and economic bondage for over a century. You were the willing vessel. Of course, certain communities will rebel. Thank you for all of the jobs you created, thank you for the opportunity investment zones, thank you for a strong American dollar, thank you for increasing disposable income for black families, thank you for small business tax incentives, and thank you for unemployment being the lowest for African Americans – even surpassing Obama's presidency. The devil still wants his way; he wants lower-income Americans to be kept in bondage. He wants everyone to be in bondage of course, and he uses different tools for different communities generationally. Not one of us is better or worse than each other, and none of us is the enemy. The only enemy is the enemy of mankind. The sneaky thing about the enemy of God is that he tempts each one of us in personal ways, collectively and independently. Thank God for Isaiah 45:12, which confirms that no weapon formed against us will prosper. It is up to us to accept the blessing we are given. Sadly, many Americans did not receive the blessings God gave America through you. Shame on us as a nation. This includes the supreme court for failing to uphold and stand for the truth, both houses, the executive branch, and of course, the voters.

God forgive us and heal our land.

And so, now we pay the price with an administration that appears to echo anti-American, anti-constitutional sentiments, and we have once again become the laughing stock of the world; starting with the invasion of our southern border by criminals falsely posing as refugees; the collapse of our military, diplomatic integrity, and honor for another.

More unique to your administration was that you

addressed issues that were on the hearts of American men and women for decades without any means for redress. A few of these radical issues were:

1. China dumping imports in America – the buck stopped with you there
2. China stealing our manufacturing jobs – you restored middle income America
3. China military race with America – you controlled this
4. NATO – addressing this one-way relationship
5. Trade Agreements that pervert American interests – you vehemently spoke out against them – and pulled out
6. Border Security: You built the wall to preserve American interests at home, including security and economic prosperity for every American. This includes preserving our humanitarian refugee policy.
7. African Americans: highest job creation and lowest unemployment in decades. Prison reform bill undoing Biden's 1996 criminal law, uniting millions of families.
8. North Korea established talking relations: unprecedented in the history
9. Deregulation: you decreased corporate taxes and lowered the benchmark tax rate for the middle class.
10. Fiscal conservatism: you increased incentives to small business ownership via the SBA by easing restrictions on small business ownership, removing harsh regulations,

cutting business taxes, and encouraging entrepreneurship.

11. Your robust economy was a case in point.

I say this next piece with caution and sensitivity. I have a tremendous amount of respect for any and all humans, regardless of which party they voted for. God said in his word that we couldn't change people; we can only love them. However, this didn't stop Jesus from standing against some of the policies of the Pharisees, along with breaking most of their rules, including healing on the Sabbath. At one time, when they question him in Luke 13:10 for healing a woman who was bound by Satan for 18 years, he said, "You hypocrites! Doesn't each of you on the Sabbath untie your ox or donkey from the stall and lead it out to give it water? Then should not this woman, a daughter of Abraham, whom Satan has kept bound for eighteen long years, be set free on the Sabbath day from what bound her?"

Another time, when they were about to stone a woman to death, he took his ground. Before he replied, he looked down in the dirt and moved the mud around with some sticks before responding to their Hitler-style authority system. He said, "Let anyone among you who is without sin be the first to throw a stone at her."

I believe he was waiting to hear from the father before responding. Sometimes we need to do that. In today's society, we certainly need to do that. The personal judgment anyone may have held towards you for not being perfect is a sin in itself, and I cover that in the next pages. For now, let me just say that after you left, the country imploded into a quasi-civil war.

As I mentioned, the democratic party is not what it was 35 years ago. We now have the rise in entitlement identity politics. Pronouns are being tossed around, transgenderism is on the rise, gay marriage laws are being passed, and abortion clinics are becoming widely rampant. Radicalism is taking place, and God is being thrown out of major doctrines and vital organizations. I don't believe this is God's will for our civilization. Today's democratic party is not the democratic party during and prior to the JFK days. Furthermore, we are supposed to be the leader of peace and freedom in the world. Many nations look up to us, and today, many do not respect us. We have to deal with our civil strife and heal prior to helping other nations at this point. I will not insult the democratic party, and I have respect for some of my friends or family members who may even vote that way. I will just state that the party has changed over time to include certain threats to society that may not be apparent to the naked eye. I encourage all to examine all parts of the party before casting a ballot. What the party endorsed decades ago has become radical in orientation. We are nearing the end times if we don't change.

There seems to have been a peculiar rising of certain

15

groups in the United States.

1. The entitled
2. The rebellious
3. The privileged
4. The uninformed
5. The misinformed
6. The followers
7. The media buffs
8. The socialists
9. The enemies of the constitution
10. The unpatriotic
11. The tradition attackers
12. The statue demolishers
13. The belligerent
14. The freeloaders
15. The atheists

I miss the America I grew up in.

Some would argue that a large portion of the 2000s, which was filled with the lackluster liberal presidential years of the Clintons and Obamas, did more to cause harm to America than one could possibly repair in the same decade in terms of the national debt, printing money, and big bureaucracy. Somehow, you miraculously did that. I genuinely believe that your valuable business background, adept negotiation skills, strong business acumen, and personal bravery accounted for a large part of your success;

and America's success during your tenure. You are not a career politician, and you had your own wealth. You didn't need to send or receive cash bribes; you simply had a keen motivation to make America great again. You were the first president to not take a salary, and personally, a real estate developer. You are my hero. Considering all things that sewer and swamp DC, you came to Washington with a political plunger, and in four miraculous years, you drained the swamp successfully to the horror of some lifelong bureaucrat brats, and to the surprise of all your voter base. Congratulations, you will always be a hero for this and will go down in American history as such.

I grew up saying the pledge of allegiance for 13 years every morning in school, and I will never forget what it means to me. The American values I learned as a child stayed with me even later in life as it got more challenging and I left the United States. Just like you, I am proud to be American, where at least I know I'm free. I honor the men and women who died for me to have this freedom. Sadly, many inside America have become anti-American as we find ourselves in the era of domestic terrorism for the first time in our history. What would our founding fathers say? Regardless of our personal problems at home, we are still the best nation on earth, with God-given freedoms that no other country comes close to. We are blessed, and I thank God for America every day.

President Trump, you brought back the America I grew up in. I have always wondered about how did you do it. You are a genius. I graduated high school in 1996, and in those days, America was in a simpler time. Although we were headed to destruction with the Clintons and Obamas, we didn't have full-fledged socialism as we do now. Also, we weren't in a racial civil war. Since that time, the left has used social constructs such as critical race theory to divide and conquer the masses. Bringing back racism, reliving the past, and focusing on reparations, instead of the God-given freedom our construct allots, along with equal opportunity, is not the means to the end. What seems to be misunderstood in society today is that America was founded on an equal opportunity, not equal outcome. The latter is communism. Today, unfortunately, we have a different type left that has grown to extreme proportions that are somehow misled by the erroneous belief that the government is the best place to go to ensure their survival. This is furthest from the truth and to embrace the government as your means for survival is a one-way ticket to destruction in any country, political party, or style of governance. You understood this and, for the first time, acted on it. You were not another Washington bureaucrat who sought to steal our tax dollars and obtain glory and power. You have your own money, and you came to Washington for the people. I am not sure who else can say that.

After George Bush left the white house, we have seen a new left rise up in this country. The failure of Barack Obama's presidency was characterized by several key factors, one of which was that you did more for the African American community than he did. It appears that after Obama, you received a large portion of the African American vote, and rightfully so. As I write this letter to you, our country is drowning while our leaders are out for ice cream. I miss you very much, and I wish you were in Washington, DC, right now. America needs a powerful leader to mitigate through the debris of the 21st century. Your negotiation skills are second to none of those lifelong career politicians. And what is scariest is that they are trying to incorporate Marxist ideology in our great free country.

Addressing Racism

When I was studying for my master's degree at George Washington University, your first presidential campaign was taking place across the nation. I was enrolled at the Elliott School of International Affairs, and I had applied to some of the white house internships during that time. On-campus, I created Interview The Expert Series with Geeta Chopra, where I interviewed renowned guests from different institutions such as Brookings Institute, the FBI, and Homeland Security, etc. I would have been thrilled to interview you, and I still believe I will do so one day.

During my time on campus, it appeared as I was one of the few ardent Trump supporters on a completely liberal campus. That didn't bother me whatsoever. It isolated me at times, and ultimately, we had a debate in class where I was the only conservative individual and Trump fan. One thing I cannot fathom is how we can have the best institutions in the world, and the brightest individuals go through them and come out completely brainwashed on the other side. This reminds me of something Dinesh D'Souza said on my television show; the higher learning institutions in the United States are all left-leaning due to faulty indoctrination. The curriculums and the professors who carry them out are left in orientation, and this produces more one-sided bigotry. We need to be more open-minded to the conservative movement of America and treat everyone wit equal respect. Dinesh is South Asian, just like myself, and thankfully he understands the dilemma the left has caused our Indian community. Typically, our community is all timid people; it full of followers and not leaders. That is fine; however, there is a serious problem when it comes to their voting behavior.

Mr. President, let me apologize to you about my community. I am ashamed of the voting bloc of the Indian American community in the United States, both historically and today. Dinesh said that the average Indian in America is further to the right than Pat Robertson; however, their voting behavior reflects the opposite. Why? The answer is simple; they perhaps don't have the courage to vote according to their true values; they want to fit in when they arrive in America. I am thankful I never had this issue growing up in America. I am thankful I know the truth because it has set me free. Immigrants coming to America inherently suffer from built-in low self-confidence as they embark to a new nation, and the democratic party takes advantage of this by luring them in immediately on the grounds of the race card. It works, and it works every time.

These are voters who are socially conservative and fiscally conservative at home, yet they come to America and vote liberal because they confuse the term 'liberal' with free or modern. South Asians coming from an ironclad right-winged society that limits the freedom of women and their religious freedom erroneously equate the republican party with extreme religious and political groups in India, such as Shiv Sena and racist factions of the BJP. Analyzing the error in this thinking is beyond the scope of this book, so I will move on from this topic.

In closing, I will say that the voting behavior of the South Asian American community not only makes them trade in their conservative values and destroys their heritage, but it creates further radicalism in our country. I encourage all Indian voters to educate before casting. The conservative party in America should not be compared to or classified with the problems of the BJP.

Economic Opportunity Zones, SBA CARES ACT, Low Unemployment For African Americans

I have a tremendous amount of loyalty towards you for what you have done for our economy. This is rightfully so, for how can someone refute the good news of having a higher employment ratio unless they are against employment, economic liberty, growth, job creation, and higher GDP, lower debt, and a strong currency? Those would be the individuals who believe in taking a free lunch as was provided during the yesteryears of the Obama and Clinton eras. Resistance to your policies that promote economic independence stem from a place of being spoon-fed by prior failed big governments whether from the right or left. That is a generational curse. There is a certain sense of entitlement in various groups of people scattered across America rising up, and this breaks my heart because it kills the spirit of American economic liberty along with the American dream.

The dependency created by the Obama's and Clinton's of the world has its roots deeply entrenched in the minds of the social program's recipients. They believe it is someone else's job to feed them despite the fact that they live in the world's biggest economy backed with a constitution granting them freedoms, economic liberty, deregulation, low barriers to entry, low taxes, supported by your robust economy. I have always tended to believe that poverty is a choice in America, with few exceptions. America was founded on an equal opportunity, not equal outcome.

"If Congress can do whatever in their discretion can be done by money and will promote the General Welfare, the Government is no longer a limited one, possessing enumerated powers, but an indefinite one..."

- James Madison

Thankfully, your administration was a true pinnacle of fiscal conservatism. Never before were corporate and personal taxes at their lowest threshold; we also had low barriers to entry for small businesses coupled with low government regulation and red tape to ensure ease of ownership and sustainability to the small business owner. We have the ability to become all that we want to be! America is so truly blessed beyond belief; all we need to do is travel and live abroad for six months and then come back. I encourage everyone who has made it a lifestyle to depend on the government for survival to spend some time away from America. Don't worry; the American dollar goes far in foreign currency. You can take a few thousand with you to cover one year's worth of rent, food, utilities, and transportation in India, for example.

Again, I am not insulting anyone. I have lived in India, Canada, and the USA. I have spent several weeks and months outside of America visiting 15 different countries across Asia, Europe, and South America, including Cuba. I can say with confidence; the entire world wants we have. Everyone wants God's blessing on America. I truly believe God used you to come to deliver the truth to America.

In addition, you brought back all of the manufacturing jobs from a vicious China that is and has been prepared to overtake America militarily, economically, and socially. You have tremendous courage that others are lacking. When I visited South Korea, I got a chance to visit the DMZ line. At that time in my life, I never would have thought that a few years later, an American president would step on North Korean soil for peace talks. You have accomplished what no other has been able to. Another signature trait of your presidency is that you don't apologize for your American values, nor do I.

While living in a socialist country, I have witnessed firsthand where health care is free, and people die on waiting lists. We witnessed it in Canada during the pandemic; they could not afford to vaccinate the population as quickly as America despite Canada being socialist in political nature with the government owning the health care system! In Cuba, food is rationed so people can be equally hungry and financial handouts make up the bulk of disposable income where everyone is equally poor. These socialist countries operate the way Facebook does; it's free, the guy who owns it is rich, freedom of speech is monitored, and if you say something he doesn't approve of, you are silenced. Having lived in a socialist country, I can confirm this is exactly what takes place. The left's definition of rich in these types of government systems is 'anyone who works.' The government comes after the independent thinker and reminds them who the boss is. Socialism has demonic ties to it; it is a form of divide and rule—anyone who wants to surpass the ceiling in leaves Canada for America.

"Give me freedom or give me death."

- Patrick Henry

It's we the people, not we the government!

Government is for the people, by the people. So finally, when you arrived on the scene, America got its hope back. You were the best thing that happened to America since George Washington, Thomas Jefferson, and our other founding fathers. You understand the spirit behind the constitution, and you echo the sentiments of Thomas Jefferson, one of our most brilliant founding fathers. The Biden era ushered in the new world order, with the mark of the beast being its most defining characteristic. As Thomas Jefferson proclaimed, when government gets too big – all disaster strikes. Never before has America been on the brink of communism and total collapse as it is now. When you left, you took with you the hope in every American heart for freedom, security, and security for the future. America is no longer safe. Our borders are invaded faster than we can vet people and process them properly. Our national security has been compromised. What next? Our constitution has all but been abolished. We knew the second amendment was constantly under attack, and now we find ourselves in an era of first amendment scrutiny. How can this be? Is this the same America I once knew? I am completely and utterly heartbroken about this. I hope you have plans to come back in some form.

"A Bill of Rights is what the people are entitled to against every government, and what no just government should refuse, or rest on inference."

-Thomas Jefferson

I miss the America I grew up in.

The biggest problem in America today is ignorance. Joe Biden signed the 1996 criminal act, which prosecuted many young black men and destroyed families, and your prison reform bill reversed some of that damage, along with freeing millions of others. For an alleged racist president who is tough on crime – not bad! Also, you issued a series of pardons, many to minorities. How are so many Americans living in darkness? One major contributor that the devil uses to propagate ignorance and misinformation is the media; CNN, NBC, and ABC, etc. The left media no longer separates from fact and opinion anymore; and the right-wing side is not far behind. We are clearly a nation divided. Decades earlier, the newspapers would have a separate column for opinion, and now the entire circulation is opinion. Americans have, in the process, merged the opinion of the left with fact. In doing so, they have misinterpreted facts and been misled for the last two decades. If CNN says someone is racist – well, that must be true!

"The circulation of confidence is better than the circulation of money."

- James Madison

I have hope for the future because I have hope in God.

WAKE UP, AMERICA!

"Let him without sin cast the first stone."

-Fallible Biblical Characters

When writing this book, I prayed and asked God what to say to you. He answered through the Holy Spirit, who told me to include this chapter.

I would like to preface this by saying moving God out of the constitution is a dangerous notion introduced by the left. This is one reason why I always support the candidate on the republican ticket. I believe our leaders need godly wisdom as they lead so many people. They need to be skilled at hearing God's voice through the Holy Spirit in order to fully maximize their roles as leaders of America and as they develop policies for God's people. They should be continually praying for wisdom with prayer groups and with their families, probably more than the layperson! This country was founded upon godly inspiration and we are destroying our principles by edging God out. Only God can provide the correct insight for our leaders to restore America and the direction they need to make that happen; especially at a time like this. How have humans become so proud that we don't need God anymore?

In the old testament, God used several ordinary people to do extraordinary things. I believe God put something in them to propel them to perform miracles despite all the odds stacked against them. The word ordinary here refers to individuals who were not infallible. They had problems, shortcomings, emotions, failures, and a past just like the rest of us! Each one of these men had critical flaws, yet we expect our modern-day leaders to be perfect without sin.

Moses, whom God used to free the Israelites from slavery in Egypt; and was called the Prince of Egypt, had a plethora of shortcomings. He murdered an Egyptian, married a foreigner (a sin for his day), had a short temper, disobeyed God by striking the rock instead of speaking to it (Numbers 20), doubted God about his calling, struggled with low self-esteem, low self-confidence, fear, and anxiety, and had an identity crisis about who he was according to God; and much more. Yet, God used him to do mighty things. He not only led the Slaves to freedom; he wrote the first few books of the bible and is known in history as an undeniable hero.

Let's consider King David, who is part of the direct ancestral lineage of Jesus Christ. God used David to fight the biggest battle known to mankind. Surely everyone has heard of David and Goliath, the Philistine. David is still known as a modern-day hero, and his story is recycled throughout the world in churches, schools, pop culture, books, articles, testimonies, movies, songs, speeches, sermons, documentaries, advertisements, cartoons, and daily jokes.

Surely, his is the story we read before going to battle,

undertaking a new challenge, or preparing for combat of some sort.

However, most people don't realize that the biblically honorable King David was a man guilty of murder, adultery, cheating, lying, sexual abuse of power, rape, military crimes, deception, and many more lies to cover up his adultery. He even had a child with a woman he wasn't married to (Bathsheba). Whew! Most people, including Christians, don't know David for this; they know him as the author of the Psalm's; in particular, the 23rd Psalm, which famously reads; "Although I walk through the valley of the shadow of death; I shall fear no evil, thy rod and staff they comfort me." Psalm 84:11 is another famous scripture that says, "No good thing will he withhold from those who walk uprightly." If a present-day rapist or murderer wrote those psalms, would we still read them with comfort and honor?

"You, therefore, have no excuse, you who pass judgment on someone else, for at whatever point you judge another, you are condemning yourself because you who pass judgment do the same things."

-Romans 2:1

If we consider Gideon and Jeremiah, we will be surprised to understand the depths of low self-confidence and doubt each man had. Gideon said his family is the least in the land, and he is the least in his family! He was so insecure that he needed not one but two signs from God with the dry fleece and the dew. "God, if it is really you talking to me, give me a sign with this fleece of wool." Even after receiving a sign from God, Gideon decided that wasn't enough. The next day, he asked God for another sign. Clearly, he struggled with doubt like the rest of mankind and was no exemplary soldier; however, a wondrous significance is attributed to his unparalleled defeat of the Midianites in Judges 7. Jeremiah, the weeping prophet, said he was too young and could not speak.

Perhaps the reason why we offer grace to those biblical characters and only remember the positive impacts of their good deeds is that they are dead today. I am not sure the reason, but oddly, today, we do the opposite. We don't remember our leaders for the good they did but the shortcomings they possess, simply from being human. Your wondrous victories will never be forgotten in history with your voters.

We expect too much perfection from our leaders. We forget that they are human, and the portion of America who voted against you because they had some peculiar discrepancy with your personal life is walking down a dangerous road. "Let him without sin cast the first stone." I believe you were put in place by God to accomplish what God knew no one else would do. These voters are throwing away American security by focusing on your personal life.

They have missed the entire point of the election and are blindsided by their erroneous judgment. Meanwhile, America is sinking quickly. Satan has convinced half of America to subvert their attention from what is truly important (American security, integrity, and unity) and focus on someone's personal past, shortcomings, or fallible nature as a human being. Somehow, liberals have become more preoccupied with your personal life and their version of it rather than the welfare of America. And that is what has killed America.

"When one side only of a story is heard and often repeated, the human mind becomes impressed with it insensibly."

-George Washington

In a classical ironic twist, a good portion of these voters are classified as Christian and simultaneously support the biblical characters named above. Some churches are confused about what their values are, and I believe the 2020 elections exposed a ton of Christian hypocrisy.

We need to do what we did in the past – revere our hero's for what they did for us. Surely Moses was a hero despite his sins, for if it wasn't for him, the Israelites might have still been in slavery. God used him mightily. Similarly, if it wasn't for you, America would be light years behind, enslaved to China, NATO, and unfair trade agreements that undermine American interests with open borders and a depleted constitution. Kind David fought evil – and won, just as you did with China, North Korea, and countless other enemies America had. You broke barriers, chains, and strongholds we have had for centuries. You dared to go where no man has gone before. You are a swamp drainer. You fight for America. You understand and endeavor to protect the spirit of the constitution. In my eyes, that is how you will be remembered.

"The God who gave us life gave us liberty at the same time."

-Thomas Jefferson

The Biden Debacle

As I close this letter, I have so many unanswered questions in my heart. What happens to America now? Will Donald Trump come back in 2024? Where will our country be in 40 years? What will happen to my future children? Will the left completely abolish our Judeo-Christian values? Is God finding his way out of the constitution? Will our children still say the pledge of allegiance in school? What about the future of America's borders, safety, and our police force? Who will protect our borders? Will blue lives diminish in numbers? Will the domestic terrorists take over our cities? Who will uphold our constitution? Will we fall to Marxist socialism? Will domestic terrorists become the majority? Will our country continue to be invaded from the south? Will criminals and enemies of America continue to disguise themselves across the southern border? Most importantly, will we ever have a leader such as yourself with courage ever rise up again to position America appropriately in the face of our enemies in the 21st century? Finally, will we be a nation divided against ourselves? I pray that God restores the love and unity back into our land of milk and honey.

As I sit here, thousands of non-vetted 'refugees' from all over South America flood the southern border, some of whom are valid, while others are disguised as false refugees.

Granted, America is a country that does grant the right of asylum and the resettlement of refugees. I understand that we have humanitarian motivation behind this. Refugees are an integral part of our history and I have great respect for them as they make the arduous journey to a better life in America.

As a disclaimer, I would like to state that this is not an insult to any legitimate refugee that has come to America, nor any immigrants.

Asylum has two basic requirements. First, asylum applicants must establish that they fear persecution in their home country. Second, applicants must prove that they would be persecuted on account of at least one of five protected grounds: race, religion, nationality, political-opinion or particular social group.

Non-vetted individuals can be very dangerous to a nation. Some individuals truly are refugees, such as Cubans, North Koreans, and a few others. Mr. Joe Biden started opening our borders to migrants during the covid-19 crisis at a fragile time when the country couldn't afford to process new migrants, both physically and financially, during the covid-19 era. He not only put millions of Americans at risk for covid, crime, terrorism, and financial strain but also opened up our borders to the rest of the world. His policy read to the mind of every opportunist out there that Donald J. Trump has left, and along with his departure died the integrity (and existence) of the American border. The border situation has gotten out of control, and some might say that America appears to have no borders left. Although we are struggling with a pandemic, we welcome thousands of untested migrants into America at a time when we are trying to heal our own population. Most countries have closed their country to legal travelers due to covid-19, yet we have welcomed thousands of illegal, untested and undocumented footmen and women with children. Leaving aside the covid crisis; we have made a public statement to the world that we don't vet our refugees; which means thousands from enemy lands can now come and pose as refugees. This includes terrorists, smugglers, drug dealers, criminals, enemies, ex-deportees, and so forth. This does the true refugee to America a great disservice!

As gas prices soar, we face supply chain shortages and a shortage of American workers. Small businesses are crippled by mandates, the dollar sinks, money is printed, and the government is going on a spending spree. I ask myself, what next?

Your fiscal response was always immaculate, and you understood macroeconomics. Printing money, going on a spending spree, then weaponizing the IRS to make the rich pay seems to be the current agenda, and it is scary. Your monetary policy was well received by the stock market as the Dow Jones reached its highest point in history with you as America's leader. Our currency remained strong and domestic jobs grew stronger as you pulled out of unfair trade agreements that were subpar for Americans. Having a strong responder in Washington was the catalyst for world peace. From a societal perspective, the church has more or less been fragmented. The foundational value of scripture is distorted to suit the agenda of the times ever since the radicals have taken over. We became the laughing stock of the Taliban in 2021, and our military is challenged with vaccine mandates. We have lost our respect internationally with the current administration, and our dollar is crashing. Our borders are open, and we have become an open target for our enemies. We are entering back into free trade agreements that pervert American interests; while dealing with wage inflation at home. The government is quietly implementing a divide and rule agenda to turn us against each other while they underhandedly strip away our liberties.

God, we pray for America. Make us the breadbasket of the world again and restore our borders. Heal our land and remove any leaders who are not fit according to your kingdom. Cause us to love one another again. Lord, save America. We repent and come to our knees before you. Lord, we know that all things are possible with you and we believe in your glory.

Mr. Trump, America needs you desperately. I pray for your well-being, and that God continues to use you to fulfill his purpose, whatever you pursue. In Christianity, it is said that those who hear directly from God and obey him will be used mightily by Him. Please come back to finish what you started and to 'Save America 2024.'

God bless you. And God bless America.

Your supporter,
Geeta Chopra